Hardcore Sales and Marketing
Sound Wisdom with Proven Success

by Dustin Vaughn Warncke

Legal Disclaimer

The information contained in this eBook is for informational purposes only. The author is not a lawyer or an accountant. Any legal or financial advice that is given is solely the opinion of the author based on his own experiences. You should always seek the advice of a professional before acting on something that has been published or recommended.

The material in this guide may include information, products or services by third parties. Third Party Materials are comprised of the products and opinions expressed by their owners. As such, the publisher does not assume responsibility or liability for any Third-Party material or opinions.

The publication of such Third-Party Materials does not constitute my guarantee of any information, instruction, opinion, products or services contained within the Third-Party Material. The use of recommended Third Party Material does not guarantee any success and or earnings related to you or your business. Publication of such Third-Party

Material is simply a recommendation and an expression of the author's own opinion of that material.

No part of this publication shall be reproduced, transmitted, or sold in whole or in part in any form, without the prior written consent of the author. All trademarks and registered trademarks appearing in this guide are the property of their respective owners.

Users of this guide are advised to do their own due diligence when it comes to making business decisions and all information, products, and services that have been provided should be independently verified by their own qualified professionals. By reading this guide, you agree that the author, Dustin Vaughn Warncke and Warncke Enterprises is not responsible for the success or failure of your business decisions relating to any information presented in this guide.

Live in Abundance

This is my 8th book overall. Much has been
written on the topic of sales and marketing
and this is certainly not a complete guide to
everything there is to know. These are the
best ideas, tips, and overall wisdom I have
learned over the past 20 years to be
successful in my craft of sales and
marketing, both as a career and as a side
hustle.

Over the years, I have learned how to eat
lunch in my truck, been turned down and
rejected countless times and had successes
and failures, both in grand proportions.

Through it all I have learned to trust in the
plan God has for my life and live with
purpose, meaning and significance in all I
do. I believe we exist as humans to learn to
love deeply and acquire knowledge as our
two primary needs and purposes.

I created this eBook as a guide to some
things that I have done that have worked
well in the work I have done over the years.

All tools and tactics here. No BS "methods" that seem to be taught by the endless social media advertisement sales gurus out there.

This is not a "get rich quick" publication. Instead, I am offering some timeless ideas to help you in your journey of making business deals work for you.

I, like many writers on the subjects of sales and marketing, started from scratch. Nothing. No silver spoon, trust fund or handouts. When I was 22 years old and a college graduate, my stepfather gave me a tape set of Brian Tracy's *Psychology of Selling* program. And I have been hooked on this subject of how people buy products and services ever since.

My goal here is to share some of the best tactical and practical advice I have used to close deals - lots of them. In exotic hoofstock live sales (AKA "deer trading"), a selling niche I have excelled in over the years, an average ticket is $6,000 to $12,000 for a load of animals without breaking a sweat and those are common transactions on a weekly basis.

There are some big wins and losses alike in the deer trade and you must move with the proverbial punches and stay off the ropes or you will get eaten alive, so to speak, in that business.

The one thing I have learned through all of my business dealings, especially deer trading, is that there is no shortage of money in this world. Some people may not have a lot of money and complain often about their mounting debt and past due bills.

The customers that have money to spend in abundance typically don't complain about their money problems because they usually don't have a lack of it at any time. While not every business has a client list with lots of cash reserves at hand, the truth is there is opportunity waiting for all of us.

The point in all of this is that there is no reason to live in scarcity. Live in abundance. Always be thankful to God for your future favor, grace, and mercy.

Imagine taking a teaspoon of water out of the ocean. The ocean water is the pool of available resources, such as money, and the teaspoon is your portion. Using that analogy will teach you that there is plenty of opportunity for everyone. There is enough out there for you to have more than enough, especially in the USA.

Furthermore, I have learned to go where there is abundance, not scarcity, when I am both selling and marketing. Sure, not every client is a "whale" but I have learned to deal with people that want to deal with me and have the means to do so.

Target your efforts where they make sense. Go where the money is waiting for you. Don't waste your time where there is little to no opportunity or where the money isn't plentiful. Both abundance and scarcity are contagious after all.

Two things I warn about in my work is the "Disease of More" and the "Disease to Please" and, while I want everyone in business to do well, I don't want possessions ("stuff") and achievement in an effort to please others, to ruin them.

Don't get caught up in serving everyone but yourself and lock on to having to have the next thing and the next thing better and better. That race for "more" and the approval and validation of others never seems to end. Both of those are "highs" that go on perpetually. You really can't please everyone, and you certainly can't be everything to everyone. Let go of that.

Be at peace. Take life as it comes and have reasonable, healthy goals but don't obsess yourself with the next thing to acquire or accomplish. Your health and sanity are far more important.

My prayer for your life is to live happy and healthy with positive goals and a great mindset. The rest, more often than not, will take care of itself. The resources and tools to better your situation are all around you. Tap into them. Don't stray from challenge, get in front of it. As Jim Rohn taught in his lifetime of work, "Grow bigger than your problems." We grow from our struggles and there is a lesson in every circumstance.

As always, thank you for picking up this book and reading my work. Remember, you are blessed to be a blessing.

Many Blessings to You and Yours,

Dustin Vaughn Warncke

Positive Thinking: I Like Myself!

We often neglect how important self-talk and positive affirmations impact our daily lives. We must stay positive if we are to attempt to keep other people on the positive track emotionally. And that translates well into the sales and marketing world through our resulting actions as well as those of the customer. When I teach others about positive thinking, I start by having them say two phrases I learned from that Brian Tracy tape set some 20 years ago:

"I Like Myself!"
and
"I Feel Terrific!"

Say these to yourself three times in a row each day, out loud, and you will most likely feel better about yourself, no matter what you are going through in life right now.

Positive self-esteem and positive mindset are crucial in successful living. We all have self-talk as humans. The question that remains is the content of your inner thoughts. Are they helping or harming your future?

These simple affirmations may seem elementary, but I can't tell you how many business people who sell and market for a living sabotage a sale, or many, and their own success by stringing along with a negative attitude, poor self-talk and an overall negative internal dialogue. You can't fly with eagles if you are too busy picking from a dead animal carcass with the buzzards.

Be careful of who and what you surround yourself with and remember, mindset is a good percentage of the battle. Have some positive realizations and affirmations internally about things going well. Visualize success and what you want that to be.

Ask yourself, "What do I want to be true in my life?" and set goals to achieve that. No goals? I can predict your progress and trajectory pretty quickly if you don't have any and it's not because I have a crystal ball. Success leaves a breadcrumb trail behind it about what to do and not do. Key in on those clues and let them teach you better ways to do and not do things.

Success Trajectory is Determined by Direction More Than Speed

We have all heard that part of success is taking massive action but remember this, one of the most important things I have been taught about business and life: Direction is more important than speed. Don't be so hard on yourself. Do your best. Give your best effort. Lead with significance and passion in what you do. But also give yourself some grace and mercy along the way.

We are all human after all. We are all flawed. We all fall short sometimes. The strong willed get up and try again.

Give your situation and overall outlook on life some grit and gumption. Life is not supposed to be easy. It wasn't ever designed that way. Rise to the occasion and take the proverbial bull by the horns in your life.

There are books, podcasts, videos, and blogs dedicated to visualization and positive affirmations. My point is to surround yourself with some great motivators and don't major in minor things. Listen to streaming videos and audios from the greats like Zig Ziglar, Les Brown, Jim Rohn, etc. Social media is full of this kind of inspiring content.

Stay motivated and surround yourself with winners in what you watch, read, and listen to daily so you don't get bogged down with the evening news and all the crap getting dumped out in the world. After all, isn't it true that we become what we think about, most of the time? Good food for thought.

Sales Wisdom

After I struggled for years not closing many deals, I finally learned the skills that sold the products and services in the businesses I served. The basic key to doing well in sales is following up, sometimes relentlessly, on a regular basis and using the right system to close deals as a consistent habit. These two characteristics alone are what has made me great at closing deal after deal and being the oil that lubricates the business sales engine.

There is a formula in just about every business that makes deals work. After you figure that out for your own business, simply rinse and repeat. I am considered by most one of the nicest guys you will meet but I am in relentless pursuit of my goals and hardcore selling big-ticket deals. I don't give up easy and I play to win every day.

Get After It! Success Doesn't Come to Those Who Wait Around

Are you playing the game to win on the field or simply throwing the ball on the sideline? To achieve at high levels, you must play on the field and play to win every day. No exceptions. Sure, we all have off days but people that succeed in sales practice habits that win more often than not. It is said that success is never owned, it is rented - and the rent is due every day. Why is it then that so many business professionals I have worked with in the past live with an attitude that success will come to them just by playing a decent, sometimes sloppy, game?

Life doesn't give you what you want or even what you need, it gives you what you deserve. Don't miss that. You get out what you put in. There is no other way that it works. A pile of money doesn't just magically find its way to your front door if you hope for the best. If you put in "whatever" action, you are bound to get "whatever" results.

You reap what you sow in the field. Nothing more or less. Taking massive action and making plenty of contacts, pitches, follow ups, and closes is crucial for success. Don't play a soft game.

Play the game to win every hour of every day. Achievement at high levels takes action at high levels. It is important to not burn out on winning in life. But if you keep your passion and significance first, you will have purpose to keep moving forward, regardless of what happens to you.

> Don't wish it was easier wish you were better. Don't wish for less problems wish for more skills. Don't wish for less challenge wish for more wisdom.
>
> Jim Rohn

Generating Leads

Where to find your ideal customer is different in every industry but the key I have found is to go where the money is and if that means spending money on a lead generation or an appointment setting service to get leads inbound to you, that is a good strategy to use in some cases.

Spending money on some paid social media advertising can also be a good strategy if it makes sense. Think of it as an investment to meet a prospect – kind of like a dating app.

Facebook Groups and other no-cost social media platforms are a start if you want to begin there but keep in mind that if it is free to use, much like public transportation, the city bus gets crowded with lots of people and things get trashed-out quickly from all the free public use. By that I mean that if it is a free, not paid platform or campaign, it usually gets noisy fast and the competition for what you sell can be fierce.

If everyone gets a free ride, don't expect a premium voice and great attention to your message. So don't be a cheapskate. Start with some small paid campaigns to test the water and scale up from there if that makes sense for your business.

Be Aware of How People Buy and
Sell to Their Hearts, Not
Their Minds

If you are in sales and marketing for your business in any role, you are in the people business and people usually buy with their hearts. How you make people feel, as they are the hero in the story, is vitally important to your success.

I have "sold to eat" most of my adult career and started selling sports and movie star autographs at the tender age of 12 years old under the guidance of my stepfather, who did the same type of business as a sort of work-hobby.

I learned that people buy through the way they feel. Don't miss this. If they can't like you, they can't trust you, and if they can't trust you, there is no sale to be made in many cases. People won't buy what they can't like or trust unless they absolutely must make the purchase.

You want people to buy out of their own desires and needs. This is especially true in big ticket sales. When there is more at risk, you must cater to how good the decision will make the customer feel after the deal is closed and the product or service is delivered.

One of the best closes I have learned is, "How do you 'feel' about this purchase?" Asking this question will usually tell you all you need to know about any objections or desire to move forward and close the deal. More on that later in this section.

Always be selling and closing deals and you will be playing at a higher level than your competitor who is too busy drinking coffee with his buddies, complaining about how hard it is out there. You are different than that. You sell to eat and win at it. You are a champion.

Some of the Best Business Advice I Have Learned

One of the common issues in our American society that caters well to human nature is what is called "Shiny Object Syndrome" meaning we are like raccoons and striped bass and go after everything that glitters, thinking it is gold or silver (shiny objects) without much sales resistance in our minds. Internet marketing expert Zach Crawford taught me this through one of his online courses I took in 2014 when I started doing affiliate marketing. The best piece of sales and business advice I received from that course is this: **BE THE ONE SELLING THE SHINY OBJECTS, NOT BUYING THEM!**

Don't get caught in hype. Don't sell your soul to the consumerism machine. Regardless of what you do in business, and this may sound like common sense, concentrate on selling more, beast-mode style, and, in contrast, buy softly.

This is a key I have learned in income generation and wealth building. When you have the shiny objects for sale and are not caught up in buying them, your focus shifts to making things appealing for other people and seeing the success of your buyer consuming your products or services, not your own gratification.

Now I'm not saying your needs and desires don't matter. They do. What I am saying is that if you diffuse your desire to buy everything in sight you want and concentrate on your customer's needs first, you will stand a better chance of winning long term and getting all that you want in life as a secondary reward.

You can have **everything** in life you want, if you will just help enough other people get what they want.
-Zig Ziglar

Best Selling Steps Once You Get a Meeting with a Prospect

1. Welcome: Remember, it is not all about you. The customer is the hero. Don't talk about yourself. Yes, you are important. Yes, you are a rock star, and everyone should know it, but the harsh truth is that people are more interested in listening to WII FM (What's in it for me?). Explain who you are and what you do but then pivot the message to what is in it for THEM in working with you to place business with you and make a sale.

It is true that you never get a second chance to make a first impression but don't be flashy. Be relatable. One reason I am successful is that I am transparent and can relate to buyers at their level whether it be a C-Level executive or Joe Bob, the custodian. Both buyers get treated very well in our interactions. This goes back to the old saying of treating everyone like a million-dollar customer.

People like me and trust me, more often than not, the first minute they meet me and they will tell you that if you asked them. I am more concerned about their success, not making a deal for my own needs and desires.

Do what you can to establish trust early with third party testimonials and referrals, media content like photos or videos showcasing your past work, and other trustworthy actions. Get them to think of you as "their guy" for whatever you are selling. You are on their side and are there to help them get what they need or desire. Whenever the customer thinks of your product or service, they should be thinking of you first as the guy that makes things happen in that world, you stud muffin!

2. Determine: What is Wanted or Needed?: Ever ask yourself the question if people are buying for your reasons or theirs? Keep in mind that people tend to lean on their own reasons for their buying motive. What is THEIR motivation? What is YOUR USP

(Unique Selling Proposition) to meet THEIR DBM (Dominate Buying Motive)?

This part may seem like complicated sales acronyms but it's pretty simple. As Zig Ziglar once said, "If you aim at nothing, you will hit it every time." Get to the root of what is desired or needed from your customer. Find out what makes their motor run. Motivated buyers are more likely to be a fast close. It is up to you to find out what makes the deal work in each case you encounter.

3. Select Product and Present/Build Value: "If you don't know, it won't happen." This phrase came from my first book I wrote while I was still in college 20 or so years ago and the statement rings so true today. If people don't know about what is available and how it can help them, you are leaving some, if not all, of the money on the table. Find what works best for THEIR needs, not what makes you a bigger paycheck. People are usually pretty intuitive these days and can see if you are trying to make a deal for your own needs instead of theirs.

Life insurance is a good example of this. When I needed a low-cost term life policy, I noticed almost every agent I met with at the time wanted to sell me whole or universal life because it makes more money for them. Sure, there are some benefits of these two policies but profit for the agent is one of the main reasons I've been presented these options from what I have found out later. If it makes sense to offer it and it is beneficial, that is understandable, but integrity is key in sales.

You must be trusted after the sale or it can come back and haunt you in ways you never expected. There are good reasons why vehicle and insurance salespeople get bad reputations due to what some of them have done to make a deal happen.

Build value in what you sell. Features and benefits are great but demonstrate VALUE at all times. Building up to a close with all that a customer gets for their dollar is key here. Added value, perceived discounts and other high points of your presentation are crucial here. Remember, people buy for THEIR reasons, not yours.

Cover objections head on and answer frequently asked questions in your presentation. Get everyone agreeable and they will most likely stay agreeable through the close. Get them saying "YES" and lead them down a path of least resistance. Remember, no one likes the sales process to be complicated or difficult. Make buying what you are selling as easy and fast as possible.

4. Create a Proposal with Value and Purpose: I always try
to lead with a written proposal and be transparent in all I do. No one likes surprises in the sales process, especially when it comes time to write a big check or pull out a debit/credit card or other payment method. Put everything in writing.

Stay on the same page with your prospect. People appreciate transparency, clarity, and following the understanding of what they are getting into on a transaction. This is especially true in big ticket purchases: a car, a house, land, a boat, etc.

As I mentioned above, give lots of perceived value without giving away the farm. The best proposals engage the customer/client to move forward. The worst make them ask lots of questions and feel uneasy about working with you. Spell it out. As marketing expert Donald Miller says on his podcast and in his books, "If you confuse, you lose" and you can take that wisdom to heart as it is true most of the time.

5. Close the Sale: One of my favorite closing methods is the "dipstick test" which is like checking the oil level in a motor vehicle. Gauge interest and favorability or disinterest quickly by asking some qualified closing questions such as:

"What other questions can I answer, or other information can I get you?"

"Would you like to move forward with this?"

Simply: **"Can we do this?"**

And my favorite of all time:

"How do you feel about doing this?"

As we talked about earlier, this should uncover what you need to do in order to close the sale. Don't get bogged down in negativity and beat up by objections. Again, be agreeable.

If they tell you the price is too high, don't discount it right away, if you even can. Add value and agree that it is a good deal and in their best interest. Make them feel like they are coming out a winner, not, in any way shape or form, being taken advantage of at all.

Remember, THEY are the hero, not you. We always want a win-win scenario in sales, but a customer's perception is their reality to them, like it or not.

The one phrase that has sold more for me that just about any other is, "How do you feel about this?" As we've established, people buy with their hearts, not their brains. Since, as I just touched on, perception happens to be reality for most people, we must make the perception FEEL favorable – like we are taking good care of getting the customer what they need and desire first.

Another Zig Ziglar quote is true here, "People don't care how much you know unless they know how much you care…" Brilliant, isn't it?

Sales Objections: What to Say When the Going Gets Tough!

I have "sold to eat" for a living nearly all of my adult life. Most of that time, I have been on straight commission and you either sink or swim when you have that kind of agreement with the company you serve. You only proverbially eat what you kill. It is said that a salesperson with low closing skills has skinny kids. There is some truth to that. If you want to be successful, you have to close business on a consistent basis.

One phrase I frequently use when price is a hard objection and I can't get anywhere in gaining positive traction is, "I don't have any more money to give you in this deal..." - a phrase I learned from studying sales guru Grant Cardone. This phrase changes the dynamic of the conversation and has worked for me in difficult situations time and time again.

When you start talking about "giving money away" in a deal, it signifies that you are doing the best you can with price without begging the client to take the offer and close the deal. You are standing your ground. The ball is in their court at that point to walk away or take your offer.

This may sound harsh but it's really not. A fact I learned about human nature many years ago rings true here. If they can dish it out, they can probably take a dose of it too. In other words, if someone holds you up with objections and is a hard case to deal with, chances are they can take some resistance on your end not to cave in on the price or other factors as well.

Remember, it is true that nothing happens until a sale takes place. With these ideas in practice, you should be on your way to making things happen in sale after sale. Now go sell something and help create a job for someone out there by the work you do!

A LOT OF PEOPLE BECOME DISCOURAGED TOO SOON. THE NAME OF THE GAME IS, YOU'VE GOT TO BE RELENTLESS.

-Les Brown

Marketing Wisdom

Decide How You Want to Market

The basics of marketing revolve around how you want to approach your effort in the space you are in, regardless of what you are selling.

There are three basic choices: Present, Competitive or Dominant.

Some of the customers I have served over the years just want to be known and seen as an option in the marketplace.

Others want to go after existing business out in the marketplace and compete at a high level for it.

Then there are yet others wanting to market hardcore and throw a lot of skin in the game at a high level, dominating the space they are in and seeking to win the most market share.

All of these are important and require different levels of marketing budget and effort.

The key here is to decide what you want and devise a plan to get it. Remember this fact though: It is hard to have champagne taste with a beer budget in marketing. Therefore, don't show up wanting to dominate your space if you don't bring the dollars necessary to make even being present in your market happen.

After all, you can invest truckloads of cash on your efforts and see diminishing levels of return. Spending your time and money in the right places is the key point in this scenario.

Most of my marketing clients over the years would love to have the dominate presence but simply don't have or can't spend the money it takes to win at that highest level. Choose wisely and be honest.

After weighing these options, a common and realistic response from most of my clients is they want to be present and, at the very least, competitive at a high level.

Generate Interest Where Your Customer Is Hanging Out

As I touched on earlier in the sales wisdom portion of this book, one of the places I have done the most amount of business in deer trading has been Facebook Groups I have created and maintained for a community of like-minded people with common interests. Buyers and sellers all hang out on this platform and it is a private group so we screen who gets in and boot out troublemakers.

This has been a no-cost way to generate sales and subsequent revenue for what I do but, that all being said, one must keep in mind that if it is free for you, it is for the rest of the world as well. Every Tom, Dick, and Harry competitor AND customer can find your group and, if you let everyone join it, things can get crowded, noisy, and complex in a hurry.

Much like public transportation, if everyone gets a ride, things can get run down fast. Just look at virtual garage sale type sites like Craigslist. It's a solid platform for locally selling stuff but not always the highest caliber of a customer base is hanging out on there. But it's FREE in most cases! Free has its limitations sometimes. See my point?

Therefore, where possible, some good paid ads on search engines as well as social media platforms are good to have. Go where your customers are hanging around.

These days you can pinpoint exactly the demographic and location of the customer you are looking to attract with paid ads on various platforms and read analytical feedback in real time to see how your ads are performing.

In my experience, in the decade we are living in, digital and on-demand are the spaces to play in unless you are targeting something that will be more applicable to audiences engaging in certain traditional media like print magazines, billboards on the highway or terrestrial radio and you have the budget to do so.

Traditional ads like these tend to be quite expensive and, in the case that your audience does nothing in the digital space at all, it might make sense. Engagement factors are key here.

For younger demographics though, I am a bigger fan of podcast ads, native ads on blogs and other websites, pre-roll video ads on streaming media, and other "new media" avenues. It's many times less expensive and more effective.

After all, our modern society has taught us that people want life on their terms and to watch, read and listen to things that interest them on their own time.

I say all of this to state the fact that you should study your target demographic and market where they work and play. If you are running a local business in a city catering to 50-70 year old patrons, for instance, an ad in the community newspaper might actually make sense. Here in Central Texas we have the *Community Impact* which is kind of like a tabloid size newspaper and it is well circulated and read here.

If you are targeting young hip 20-somthings, consider where they work and play. Podcasts, young social media like Tik-Tok and Instagram is where they are hanging out.

Get my drift?

I remember the last guy that delivered a hard copy of our local phone book to me and recommended I use it for rifle target practice. Good advice. That medium of media is not as relevant as it used to be by any means. Not even by a long shot.

Things have changed dramatically on how we consume media in the past two decades and that change is coming even faster at us every day. That all being said, it is important to be adaptable and get the best return on investment for your money for your marketing dollar and your efforts on any platform you choose.

Time is finite. Advertising and marketing budgets are too.

"Go where the audience is" may sound cliché and elementary but I have consulted with more than a few businesses that are running newspaper or print magazine ads trying to attract millennials to buy something. It just doesn't work like that. The target audience just isn't in that space for the most part.

Your message needs to meet your prospective people where they are engaging. It's simple but often overlooked.

The days of "spray and pray" and "hope for the best" are over. We live in the most marketed-to culture in the history of the world and human-kind. There are ads trying to sell us something everywhere we turn and on everything we tune in to these days. That is just the way of our world.

Targeting your marketing message to your defined audience is where the rubber meets the road. There are no shortcuts worth taking here. Concentrate less on LIKES and more on true engagement with your campaigns.

What are people doing in response to what you are putting out there? Are there multiple points of engagement? Is your message clear or confusing? If I met you for the first time, how would you convey your message and mission clearly and simply if we were on a short elevator ride together?

These are all questions to consider when planning your marketing strategy.

Websites: Three Important Messages of Every Landing/Home Page

When people visit your personal or company website, the home page should convey answers to three questions everyone asks: **"Who are you?" "What do you do (or) What do you sell?"** and **"How can I buy it?"**

Many sites I encounter don't do this well enough at all. Think it's too simple? If you lead with a message that is too complicated, you create a high risk of confusing and losing your prospective buyer or even a returning customer. Keep it simple and on point.

It doesn't matter how fancy your website is or how pretty it looks. You really have one opportunity to make a connection and get people to engage with you.

The old saying goes, "You never get a second chance to make a first impression," and this is so true. Be clear. Be direct.

Beating around the bush with your message only leads to customers beating around the bush to figure out who you are, what you do and how they can buy from you.

BE KNOWN and REMIND OFTEN

It is said that obscurity is the cause of many personal brand and business brand failures. If people are not told about you and reminded of who you are and what you do, it's a losing game. Play the game to win.

Build an e-mail list and send out a newsletter or e-mail update with what you offer one to two times a month at a bare minimum. Depending on your market and strategy, you may need to send communication once or twice a week or even every day.

I have worked with so many businesses that are on the track of failure due to not staying in regular contact with their "fan base" of customers and without a plan for attracting new customers.

Engaging Lead Magnets

Having a lead magnet is an opportunity for people to give you a way to contact them, especially an email or mobile phone number, and it is vitally important if you want to keep the sales coming in and your doors open.

Write up something and make it a downloadable PDF to give away that is relevant to the clients you serve in return for their contact info.

Do something of value for new and returning visitors.

These may sound like basic ideas but I run into companies all of the time that flop around like fish out of water due to not having a lead generation plan in place. Provide value in all you do. Stay in touch. Remind people you are there for them and what you offer.

This eBook is a good example of a lead magnet and can be used in many ways to generate sales. It is small, easy to digest in one sitting and can be downloaded quickly.

Of all the eBooks I have written, I haven't produced any of them for profit. They are my business card, a sales tool, and my way to share knowledge with those that wish to engage with me - nothing more and nothing less.

A roofing company might write a guide to help current and future customers with their insurance claims and to educate them on how to have the best experience in the process as possible.

An HVAC (Heating and Air Conditioning service contractor) may write a guide on energy saving tips during the hot and cold months of the year and ways to help their customer save money.

A hunting or fishing guide might write tips for having the best adventure in the outdoors on a guided trip with them or another outfitter.

The list goes on.

This is not hard for you if you haven't done something like this yet. You are just sharing your knowledge and expertise on what you market or sell to help your customer in their journey and further help them be the hero. You want them to live their best life now with your product or service. We aren't talking rocket science here.

Write some content and get some photos together, combine it in a word processing document, and convert it to a PDF. Then you can put that PDF link on a Thank You page after prospects give you their email in return for downloading your guide. Easy and simple.

If you think doing something like this is hard, hire someone to help. Give them talking points and design ideas you have. This doesn't have to be super fancy and integrating it doesn't have to be hard either.

The Three Most Important Parts of Your Marketing Message

One of my best marketing tips is to make sure you are doing three things with your audience when you are creating any type of content. Consider **relevance, authenticity,** and (most importantly) **engagement** points for your marketing message.

Without these three important factors, you risk losing your audience and, in applicable cases, critical sales volume. If you want people to engage with you, there should be clear opportunities for them to do so.

Also, if you are not being relevant or authentic, it will be evident in your success. We are more in tune as a society and can quickly sniff out BS artists and fake news.

Also, consider the fact that marketing with a good **call to action** (CTA) in multiple areas is also very important to converting casual observers and recipients of whatever you are creating into dedicated buyers.

If you are sending an email, this would also include your subject line. This is vitally important. No "weak sauce" should be allowed in your message... Anywhere. Bring your best to the table! Make it all count!

The goal in any email campaign is to stay in front of your audience and remind them you are there but also get the customer to open the email and give multiple points of engagement inside. Always lead with value here.

Most people get a ton of email and some have multiple email accounts to check. If the message and engagement points are not spot-on, a prospect or even current customer is getting ready to get "delete happy" and start pulling the trigger, deleting your email or, worse, unsubscribing from your list. At that point, getting them back is a big challenge.

When you depend on a list of new and repeat customers to come to your site to buy from you, keep in mind their buying motives.

How does buying what you offer make them feel?

Is it a need or a want they have to buy your product or service?

This will help you make better conversions time and time again and achieve true lasting success in your business.

For years, I have told my son every day when I drop him off for school to, "Make Good Choices…"

We all have choices every day in how we think, respond to tough situations, sell and market to our audience, and many other factors. Choose wisely.

Be blessed, my friends.

About the Author

Dustin Vaughn Warncke is an avid sales and marketing professional and started selling and learning buying signals and selling and marketing psychology at a young age.

In sales, Dustin has sold youth fundraising programs to schools and organizations, brokered hunting adventures all over the world, sold office supply delivery services, sold print and digital media/advertising, and done thousands of big-ticket live exotic hoofstock transactions, among other sales accomplishments.

In marketing he has built hundreds of top performing websites for local and international businesses, run email and search ad campaigns, and is proficient in several e-commerce platforms and search engine tools.

Dustin lives in Central Texas with his wife and son and is an avid outdoorsman and outdoor TV show producer along with pro-staff for several outdoor companies.

Dustin's goal is to inspire and educate others on reaching their potential and succeeding in personal and professional goals and dreams and to live their best life now.

See Dustin's other eBooks, articles, and other work at
www.dustinsprojects.com